Fun with
Paper Sculpture

Clive Stevens

SEARCH PRESS

First published in Great Britain 1998

Search Press Limited
Wellwood, North Farm Road,
Tunbridge Wells, Kent TN2 3DR

ISBN 0 85532 862 2

Suppliers
If you have any difficulty in obtaining any of the
materials and equipment mentioned in this book, then
please write for a current list of stockists, including
firms who operate a mail-order service, to the
Publishers.
Search Press Limited, Wellwood,
North Farm Road, Tunbridge Wells,
Kent TN2 3DR, England

Publisher's note
All the step-by-step photographs in this book feature
the author, Clive Stevens, demonstrating how to
create paper sculptures. No models have been used.

Colour separation by P&W Graphics, Singapore
Printed in Spain by Elkar S. Coop. Bilbao 48012

Contents

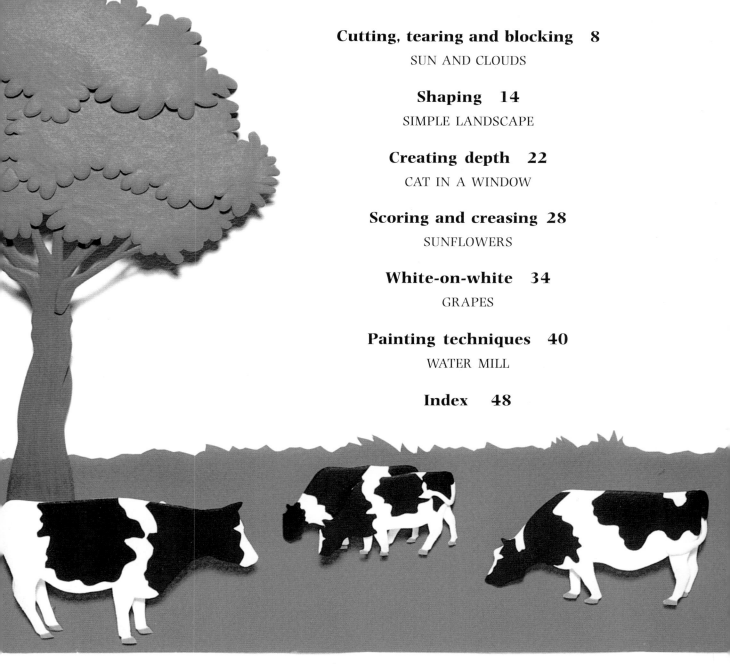

Introduction

It is believed that paper has been in existence from as early as 202BC. Attributed to the Chinese, it is said to have been invented during the Han dynasty. Due to its versatility, both as an art and craft medium, paper is probably one of the most popular and economical of all the creative materials used today. It is also quick and easy to work, without the need of specialist equipment, and with very little mess and fuss one can achieve very impressive results. It was these attributes that led me to discover paper sculpture. Although I call my art 'sculpture', it is more accurately described as bas relief, a technique which creates both actual and illusionary depth in an image.

It has always amazed me how much interest this art form has generated since my very early exhibitions. I have found myself running weekend courses for would be paper sculptors, writing books and magazine articles and even appearing on childrens' television, to demonstrate the many effects that can be achieved with paper.

This book is titled *Fun with Paper Sculpture*, and that is just how I have tried to plan it – each project teaches you an important technique that you need to master before moving on to the next project. Through careful cutting, shaping, blocking and gluing, all the projects in this book can be achieved with little or no previous experience.

Paper is available in many colours, textures and weights, although some lend themselves to shaping techniques more than others. I have found that the most versatile paper is a handmade, cotton rag, watercolour paper – it can be worked into wonderfully deep, rounded shapes, and it is also ideal for hand-coloured sculptures.

Simple line diagrams are included in each project from which you can photocopy and/or trace a working pattern. You can enlarge the diagrams to whatever size you choose. The diagram for the first project is drawn with solid and broken lines. The solid lines denote the visible edge of the shape, while the broken lines outline extension areas. Extensions are used where layers overlap each other, to allow for gluing points. You will need to remember to allow for extensions on the other projects. I have also annotated the diagrams for the first two projects in the order of assembly. Again, you will find it advantageous to adopt this habit for all future sculptures.

When you start creating your own designs, as you will undoubtedly want to, remember that you are working with an illusionary depth and that the foreground and background layers are only 25–50mm (1–2in) apart. If you wish to frame your finished piece you must work to the maximum depth of your chosen frame, otherwise, you will end up squashing your sculpture.

In every project, work forward from the background layer. In a landscape, for example, start by laying down the sky, add the distant horizon and any cloud formations, then the middle distant trees and, finally, the foreground details.

I hope you enjoy working through this book, and that you do have fun with paper sculpture. It is a very rewarding hobby and I am sure you will find that friends and family will be impressed by your efforts.

OPPOSITE

Explosion of toys

Full size section of a large paper sculture shown in full on pages 46–47. Modern papers allow you to create stunning, beautifully coloured designs.

Materials and tools

You can start paper sculpture with just a few sheets of paper, a pair of scissors, pieces of foam core board and PVA glue. However, you will soon want to start working with particular types of paper, and to create more interesting pieces. There are four basic types of paper: uncoated, coated, handmade and specialist, all can be obtained from good stationers or art suppliers. Below I describe the different types of paper and the other equipment used for paper sculpture.

Uncoated papers Most of the machine made papers used in the printing industry are in this group. They have a dull surface and are available in shades of white and cream, and a range of brighter colours. You can also buy uncoated papers that have decorative embossed finishes.

Coated papers These have a smooth finish and are generally used for high quality printing. They are available in shades of white and a wide range of bright colours. Coloured papers are usually one-sided – with colour on the front and white on the back. One-sided papers are useful, as they can be torn to leave an attractive white edge.

Handmade papers These papers are invariably made from cotton or linen rags, plants or vegetation. They are very malleable and can be worked into well-rounded shapes without breaking the fibres of the paper.

Specialist papers This group includes those papers that fall outside the other catagories, and include types such as corrugated, crepe and tracing paper.

Foam core board This is a lightweight display board that consists of a layer of foam sandwiched between card. It is available from art and craft shops in various thicknesses. For the projects in this book I use 3 and 5mm ($1/8$ and $1/4$in) foam. It is an excellent backing for paper sculpture designs, and I also use it for blocking the layers of a design. You can use silicone adhesive for blocking (see page 34), but I prefer to work with known thicknesses of material.

Glues PVA glue is used for sticking together the pieces of a sculpture. Use cocktail sticks to apply PVA glue to the foam strips.

Cutting tools A good pair of pointed scissors and an ever sharp craft knife are essential.

Draughting tools A hard and soft pencil, an eraser, a steel ruler, a set square and a compass are required when transferring designs on to paper.

Shaping tools These are used to emboss shape and texture on the cut paper shapes. There is quite a variety of tools available from craft shops, but you can also improvise by making your own from wood, plastic or metal. My favourite tool actually started life as a dentist's plaque remover. The working end of all shaping tools must be very smooth. You will need a selection of shapes: a fine pointed tool, a well-rounded one and one with a rather flat roundness to it, will be enough to get you started.

You will need an embossing mat. This must be soft enough to allow the shaping tool to work, but firm enough to support the paper without tearing. A piece of high-density foam or thick floor covering is ideal.

Painting equipment Acrylic or watercolour paints, paint brushes, an old toothbrush and a sponge are useful for creating colours and textures that cannot be found on plain papers.

Materials and equipment for paper sculpture

1. Silicone adhesive
2. PVA glue
3. Cocktail sticks
4. Shaping tools
5. Paint brush
6. Watercolour paper
7. Acrylic/watercolour paints

8. Assorted coloured paper
9. Toothbrush
10. Tracing paper
11. Steel ruler
12. Compass
13. Pencils and eraser
14. Craft knife

15. Scissors
16. Natural sponge
17. Set square
18. Foam core board
19. Cutting mat
20. Embossing mat

Cutting, tearing and blocking

Sun and clouds

In this first project I take you, step by step, through the basic techniques of paper sculpture: transferring the design to the paper, tearing shapes, cutting them with scissors and a craft knife and finally, blocking. Blocking is the technique of assembling the paper shapes on a baseboard, using strips of foam core board (hereinafter referred to as foam) to raise them off the surface to achieve illusionary depth. It is most important to transfer the pattern, in reverse, on the back of each shape. This practise will allow a little leeway when cutting round the shapes – residual pencil lines do not have to be erased, and the front surface remains crisp and clean.

I used a same-size photocopy of this diagram to produce the sculpture on page 12. The broken lines on the diagram show the extensions that must be included when the individual pieces are cut out. The numbers refer to the order of assembly.

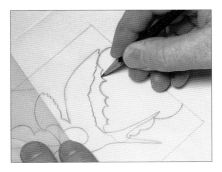

1 Use a soft pencil to trace the pattern. Draw round each shape, including all the broken lines for the extensions.

2 Place the tracing, face down, on the back of the coloured paper and use a sharp, very hard pencil to transfer the traced outline. Remember that this drawn image is the reverse of that on the pattern.

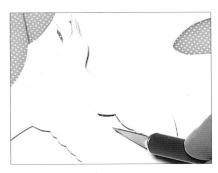

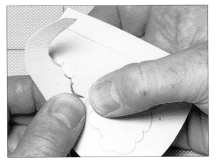

3 Use sharp scissors to cut simple shapes such as the background sky and the sun.

4 Use a craft knife to cut round more intricate shapes.

5 For shapes such as clouds, which have soft, fluffy edges, first roughly cut all round with a craft knife. Then, working with the pencilled design face up, carefully tear round the pencil line and remove the excess paper.

6 To create the black feathers on the wing tip, glue an oversize piece of black paper to the front of the wing with PVA glue. Turn the bird over and use a craft knife to cut round the shape of the feathers.

7 Number all the shapes on the tracing and then annotate the cut out shapes with the same numbers. This may seem unnecessary for a such a simple design, but it is a useful habit to adopt for more complex designs.

The background sky together with the other shapes ready to be assembled.

8 Apply PVA glue to the back of the sky, then stick it firmly on to the foam baseboard.

9 Use a craft knife and steel ruler to cut 5mm (¼in) wide strips of 5mm (¼in) foam. Trim the strips to fit each shape.

10 Use a cocktail stick to apply PVA glue to one side of a strip and glue it across the back of the cloud (shape 1). Holding the foam strip on the tip of the knife blade will stop you getting glue on your fingers.

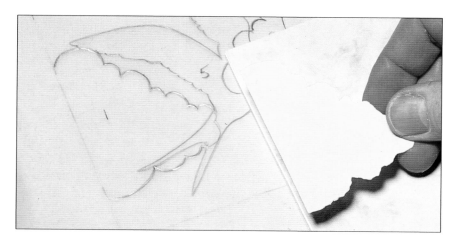

11 Apply more glue to the other side of the foam strip and then, using the tracing as a guide, glue the cloud (shape 1) to the sky.

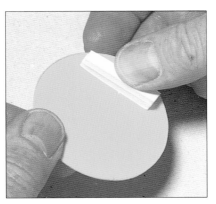

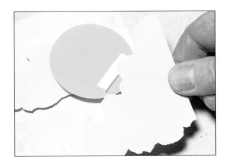

12 Repeat steps 10 and 11 for the centre cloud (shape 2). Check the position by laying the tracing over the clouds.

13 Glue two strips of foam together, then glue them to the bottom right of the sun (shape 3). Remember that you are working on the back of the paper. Use the tracing as a guide to glue the sun to the sky.

14 Glue a single strip of foam on top of the sun and then glue the cloud (shape 4) on to this strip.

15 Add depth to the bird (shape 5) by folding the front wing forward and the other wing backward.

16 Glue three short strips of foam together and then glue this triple strip to the back of the bird. Finally, glue the bird in position on the sky.

Sun and clouds

This simple project demonstrates the contrast between the soft torn edges of the clouds and the hard cut edges of the bird and sun. The basic techniques used to create this picture apply to all the projects in this book.

Finished size: 172 x 120mm (6 3/4 x 4 3/4in)

OPPOSITE:

Kite

Another simple design that features the basic techniques of cutting and blocking, and provides a good comparison between cut and torn edges.

I used uncoated papers for the sky, the clouds and the streamer, and one-sided coated paper for the kite. On this design I opted to have hard, cut edges to the clouds which are blocked on single strips of foam. I tore a sheet of one-sided yellow paper to make the complete shape of the kite, tearing the paper to give a slightly rough white edge. I then tore one-sided red paper in the shape of two triangles and glued them flat on the yellow background. I blocked the kite on two strips of foam. One end of the streamer is glued between the foam strips under the kite. The other end is bowed slightly and glued to the edge of the sky.

Finished size: 172 x 216mm (6 3/4 x 8 1/2in)

12

Shaping

Simple landscape

In this project I introduce the technique of shaping (embossing) the cut pieces of paper. Shaping changes the way light catches each piece of the design, and this creates a more realistic look.

I used brightly coloured, uncoated papers for this design. You can use your own colour scheme or follow the one I used for the finished sculpture on page 18. Again, I have numbered the shapes in the order of assembly – remember to annotate each shape after tracing it on to the paper. However, I have omitted showing any extensions – these are fairly obvious, and can be seen in the step-by-step instructions.

Check list
Uncoated papers: blue, white, light green, mid green, light brown, yellow, grey and black
Tracing paper and pencils
Scissors
Craft knife, steel ruler and cutting mat
Foam core board, 3 and 5mm (1/8 and 1/4in) thick
PVA glue and cocktail sticks
Shaping tools and embossing mat
Set Square

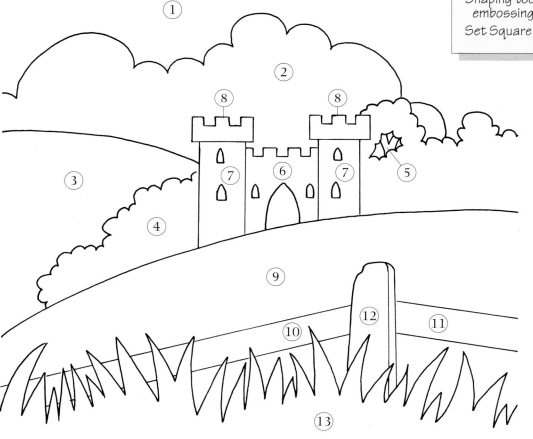

Photocopy this diagram to make a working pattern. For the sculpture on page 18, I enlarged the diagram by 150%.

14

1 Enlarge the diagram opposite to make a working pattern and then make a full-size tracing of the shapes. Transfer the outline of each shape, including all necessary extensions, on to the appropriate colours of paper and then cut them out. Note that the foliage (shape 4) extends right across the design, behind the castle, and that the cutout for the turrets (shape 7) includes a joining strip that is covered by the yellow field (shape 9). You will also need scrap pieces of black paper to stick behind the door and windows of the castle.

Front of cloud after step 2.

2 Place the cloud (shape 2) face down on an embossing mat. Use a pointed tool to emboss a crease round the edges.

3 Now, working gently but firmly, use a well-rounded tool to soften the inside of the embossed edges.

Front of cloud after step 3.

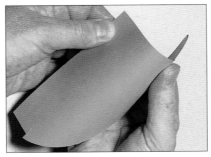

Front of cloud after step 4.

4 Shapes such as clouds have lots of depth, so use a flat, rounded tool to soften and shape the central area of the cloud.

5 Shapes such as the rolling distant field (shape 3) can be worked over dowelling or a long smooth modelling tool. Try to create a gentle curve from the bottom to the top of the piece.

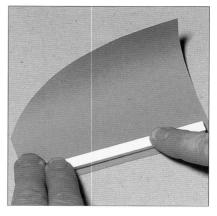

6 Glue the sky (shape 1) flat on the baseboard. Apply a line of glue along the bottom extension of the cloud (shape 2) and glue it to the sky, using the tracing as a guide (see page 10). Bend the cloud up slightly to make its top edges stand clear of the sky.

7 Glue a strip of 5mm (¼in) foam across the bottom edge of the distant field (shape 3).

8 Glue a short strip of 5mm (¼in) foam to the back of the foliage (shape 4) as shown. Glue the tree trunk (shape 5) across the gap in the foliage.

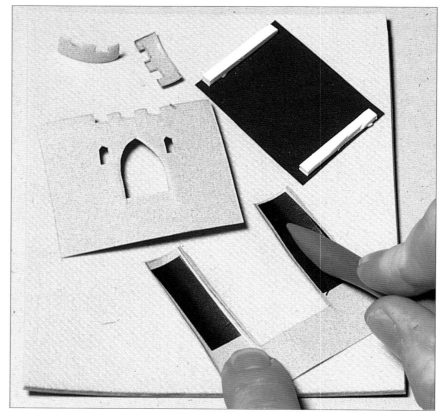

9 Glue the distant field to the baseboard so that its top edge contacts the cloud. Glue the foliage to the baseboard so that it stands clear of the cloud.

10 Use a well-rounded tool to curve the turret tops (shapes 8). Cut a piece of black paper slightly smaller than the front of the castle (shape 6) and stick a strip of 3mm (⅛in) foam down each side. Stick pieces of black paper behind the windows in the turrets and then use the well-rounded tool to shape the turrets.

11 Glue the front of the castle (shape 6) to the two strips of foam on the black paper. Glue the bottom joining strip of the turrets (shapes 7) directly to the front of the castle. Glue the turret tops (shapes 8) directly to the turrets and then glue the complete castle over the foliage. Remember to use the tracing to check the position.

12 Cut two long strips of 5mm (¹/₄in) foam, stick them together and then glue this double strip across the bottom edge of the baseboard. Assemble the foreground field (shape 9) on this strip and use a set-square to ensure that field is square to the baseboard.

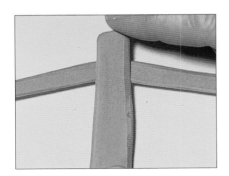

13 Shape the three pieces of the fence (shapes 10, 11 and 12) to give them a three-dimensional appearance. Glue strips of 5mm (¹/₄in) foam to the back of each piece, then assemble the fence directly on top of the foreground field.

14 Glue two single strips of 5mm (¹/₄in) foam across the bottom of the foreground field as shown, positioning them directly over the double strip underneath the field. Shape the strip of grass (shape 13) – curve some of the blades inwards, others outwards – then glue the strip across the bottom of the picture.

Simple landscape

The bright colours used on this design give form to the landscape. A good sense of depth has been created with just a few shapes by having clearly defined background, mid-ground and foreground areas. Compare the effect of the shaped pieces on this sculpture with that of the flat ones in the first project on page 12.

Finished size: 200 x 215mm (8 x 8 ¹/₂in)

A sunny day

The shaped roof tiles and rows of flowers add visual interest to this otherwise very simple design.

Finished size: 115 x 95mm (4¹/₂ x 3³/₄in)

A stormy day

The shaped clouds add interest to this version of the design used for the sculpture above. The high blocking of the clouds casts deep shadows to help reinforce the stormy theme.

Finished size: 115 x 95mm (4¹/₂ x 3³/₄in)

Teddy bear

Teddy bears are always favourite subjects. Here I have made up a background of sky, clouds and grass, over which I glued a picture mount. I then created the bear and glued him on top of the mount.

Finished size: 172 x 172mm (6 ³/₄ x 6 ³/₄in)

OPPOSITE

Flight path

This picture owes its overall effect to the use of bright colours and very simple shapes. The white vapour trails add contrast and make the colours more vivid.

Finished size: 160 x 215mm (6 ¹/₄ x 8 ¹/₂in)

Creating depth

Cat in a window

This project shows one way of creating lots of illusionary depth to a picture. The design is basically two views – a background and a foreground, separated by a blocked up mount which acts as the wall of a house. (A simpler version of this idea is shown on page 21).

The background landscape is assembled in the same way as the one on pages 14–18. The foreground uses a folding technique to create curtains that add a sense of realism to the window. The cat asleep on the window sill adds a focal point to the overall design.

Once again, I have used uncoated papers for all the shapes, with a plain linen-effect paper for the curtains. You could also use a fine patterned paper for the curtains. Begin by cutting out all the pieces and numbering them.

Another way of creating depth is by the subtle use of different scales. An example of this method is shown on page 27.

A simpler version of this idea is shown on page 21. The background landscape is assembled in the same way as the one on pages 14–18. An example of this method is shown on page 27.

Check list
Uncoated papers: pink, mauve, orange, yellow, blue, white, mid green, dark green, cream and black
Tracing paper and pencils
Scissors
Craft knife, steel ruler and cutting mat
Foam core board, 3 and 5mm ($^1/_8$ and $^1/_4$in) thick
PVA glue and cocktail sticks
Shaping tools and embossing mat
Set Square

Enlarge this diagram to an appropriate size to make a working pattern. Use this project to test your ability to number the shapes in the order of assembly. When cutting out the paper for the curtains, allow for the folding. Remember to include necessary extensions on other shapes.

1 Assemble the background scene on to the baseboard. Leave space on all four sides of the baseboard to allow for the blocking of the wall of the house.

2 Build a four-sided frame around the edge of the background scene using double strips of 5mm (¹/₄in) foam.

3 Cut the wall, with a window opening, out of a sheet of 5mm (¹/₄in) foam – allow space at the sides of the opening to mount the window frames. Glue wallpaper to the wall.

4 Apply glue to the blocking strips on the baseboard and carefully lay the window opening over the top. Hold in place for a minute or two to allow the glue to set.

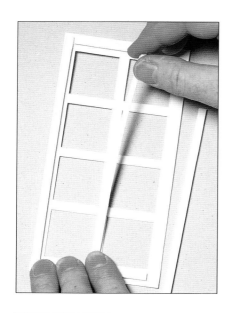

5 Carefully cut out the window frames with a craft knife. Ensure that all corners are clean and square. Strengthen the back of the frames with strips of 3mm ($^1/_8$in) foam.

6 Apply glue to the top, bottom and outside edge of each frame, check their positions with the traced pattern and then glue them to the wall.

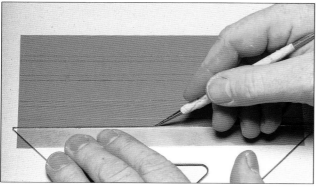

7 Use a pointed tool and a set square to score the folds in the curtains. Vary the spacing between the folds to create a natural appearance.

8 Make the first wide fold by hand, creasing the folded edge between finger and thumb.

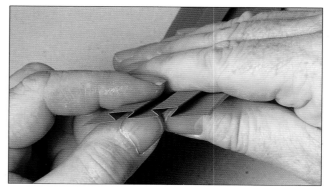

9 Use a set square, placed along the next scored line, to help make the narrow fold.

10 Continue working the folds across the piece of paper to create a folded curtain as shown. Repeat steps 7–10 for the other curtain.

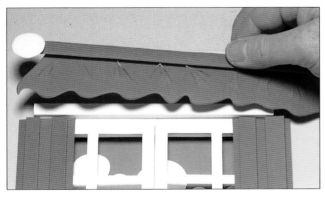

11 Glue the curtains at the top of window frame. Assemble the pelmet, gluing a 5mm (¼in) foam strip between the rail and the frill. Glue a double foam strip to the wall, above the frame, then glue the assembled pelmet to this strip.

12 Glue a double 5mm (¼in) foam strip to the back of the bottom part of the window sill and carefully fold the top part back at a slight angle. Glue the window sill to the wall so that its top edge slides under the bottom of window frame.

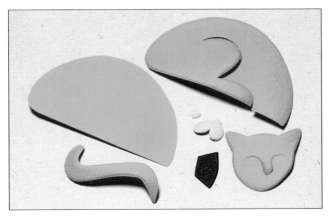

13 Cut out and shape the cat components. Notice that there are two body shapes, one cut round the shape of a rear leg. On the face shape, use a craft knife to cut the outline of the top of the eyes and the nose.

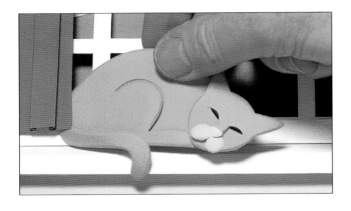

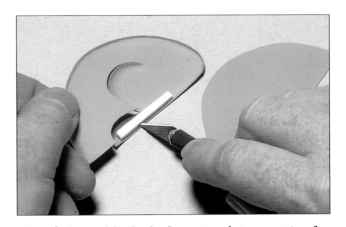

14 Assemble the body parts, gluing a strip of 3mm (⅛in) foam so that the leg sits slightly proud of the body. Assemble the rest of the cat, sliding the small black piece under the nose to leave a fine black line for the closed eyes.

15 Glue a short 5mm (¼in) foam strip to the back of the cat and glue the finished cat to the window frame and sill.

Cat in a window

The finished sculpture has a good sense of depth through the use of the multi-blocking. You could use this principle and make many variations of the basic design.

Finished size: 305 x 305mm (12 x 12in)

OPPOSITE

Cat on a dustbin

This cat is wide awake waiting for the dustmen to call. He is made in the same way as the sleepy one above. This design is given the illusion of great depth through the use of scale – note that the garden gate, which has been left open to invite you into the picture, is actually much larger than the house.

Finished size: 190 x 310mm (7 1/2 x 12 1/4in)

Scoring and creasing

Sunflowers

Flowers and foliage are excellent subjects for paper sculpture. This vase of sunflowers is a perfect project to demonstrate the technique of incising (scoring and creasing), to add to your paper sculpting repertoire. The flower heads are shaped as normal and then a vein is incised down the centre of each petal.

Although the petals overlap on the pattern, cut and assemble them as complete flower heads. Each flower head is slightly different but there are only two basic sizes. The background is made with two colours of paper; one covers the whole of the baseboard and a smaller piece is glued across the bottom. The vase is made up in the same way. Extensions are required on the stalks so that they extend from the centre of a flower head to the middle of the vase.

Enlarge this diagram to an appropriate size to make a working pattern.

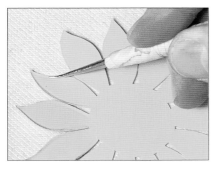

1 Use a craft knife to cut out all the flower heads, then define the edges of each petal with a pointed shaping tool.

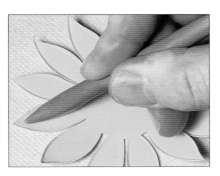

2 Use a well-rounded tool to create a curve on each petal.

3 Now use the pointed tool to score a line through the middle of each petal.

4 Turn each flower head over and finish shaping petals by creasing the scored lines between finger and thumb.

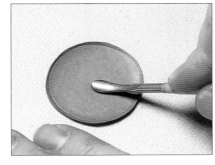

5 Cut out all the seed heads. Use the pointed tool to define the outer edge, then use a flat rounded tool to emboss the seed head into a shallow dome shape.

6 Cut some short strips of 5mm (¼in) foam and use these to assemble the seed heads on the petals.

7 Cut out the stalks, define their outer edges with the pointed tool, then use a well-rounded tool to create a curved shape.

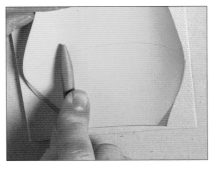

8 Define the outer edges of the two-tone vase, then use the well-rounded tool, working from side to side, to create the impression of a curved surface.

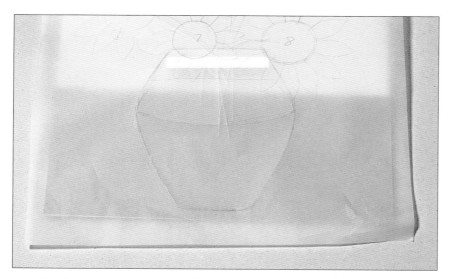

9 Cut three strips of 5mm (¼in) foam, slightly shorter in length than the width of the top of the vase, and glue them together as a thick strip. Use the tracing as a guide and glue this thick strip to the background just below where the top of the vase will be.

10 Use the tracing to mark the centres of the flower heads on the background. Glue the stalks on the foam strip and, when dry, trim off any excess.

11 Glue a single strip of 5mm (¼in) foam across the bottom of the vase, then glue the vase to the background. The top of the vase will angle outwards, resting on the stalks.

12 Use two, three and four thickness foam strips to position the top of each stalk at a different level.

13 Finally, glue the flower heads in position – some directly on their stalks, some raised on short foam strips. The bottom-left flower head is glued to the top of the vase with a single strip of foam.

Sunflowers

The finished sculpture is reminiscent of Van Gogh's Vase of Sunflowers. Blocking each flower head at a different height and the petal veining creates great depth and hence some interesting shadows.

Finished size: 268 x 375mm (10 1/2 x 14 3/4in)

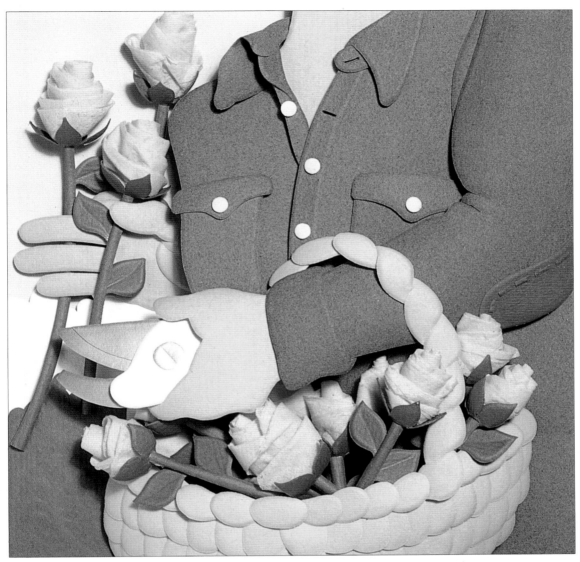

Gathering roses

Uncoated paper is used to create most of the shapes in this unusual design. However, the roses are constructed from pink, soft tissue paper carefully wound and glued together, while silver foil coated paper is used for the blades of the pruning shears and the pivot. The basket is made from shaped ovals glued to a flat former (see the grapes on page 36). The handle is made in a similar way.

Finished size: 150 x 150mm (6 x 6in)

OPPOSITE

Floral display

Study the construction of different flowers and you will soon see how you can create them from paper. This vase of assorted flowers is made from a wide range of splendidly coloured, uncoated paper.

Finished size: 260 x 360mm (10$^1/_4$ x 14$^1/_4$in)

White-on-white

Grapes

White-on-white is considered to be the purest form of paper sculpture. Shape and depth is created simply through the use of light and shade. I have devised this project of grapes on a trellis to introduce this subject. The whole design is worked using handmade, cotton rag, watercolour paper.

White-on-white work can be ruined if the paper becomes marked. Keep your hands clean and dry, and make sure you do not get pencil marks on the front of the paper.

The incising technique is used extensively in this project to detail the vine stems and leaves, and the wood grain on the trellis.

Another deviation from normal practice is the use of silicone adhesive for blocking the grapes. Individual grapes are shaped and then attached to a former with small blobs of silicone adhesive. This adhesive allows them to be attached at an angle to help create the illusion of bulk in the bunch.

Enlarge this diagram to an appropriate size for a working pattern. Note that the individual grapes are assembled on to a paper former that must be cut slightly smaller than the outline of the whole bunch.

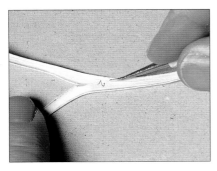

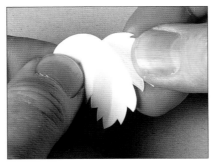

1 Cut out the eight complete lengths of trellis. Cut the vine stems as long lengths – there are three separate stems entwined in the trellis. Use a pointed shaping tool to score a grain pattern on the front face of the trellis and stems. Turn the pieces over and define their outer edges.

2 Cut out the individual leaves. Note that only five of them have stems attached. Score veins on each leaf, some on the front, others on the back. Use the pointed tool to define the edges, then carefully crease along the scored veins to create a three-dimensional effect.

3 Use a well-rounded shaping tool to create curls on the tips of some of the leaves.

Full-size pieces that have been scored, creased and shaped as described in steps 1–3. The individual grapes are shaped in the same way as the sunflower seed head on page 29. Only thirty-seven grapes are visible on the pattern, but you will need to cut a few more to help create a three-dimensional effect.

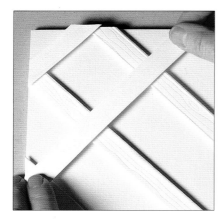

4 When all the pieces have been shaped, start to assemble the picture. First, use PVA glue to attach a sheet of paper to the baseboard and then, using strips of 3mm ($^1/_8$in) foam, glue the lower four lengths of trellis to the background. Use more strips of 3mm ($^1/_8$in) foam and glue the upper lengths at right angles to and on top of the lower lengths.

5 Entwine the branches through the trellis and secure them at convenient places with small amounts of PVA glue.

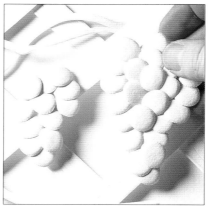

6 Use blobs of silicone adhesive to assemble the individual grapes on a paper former. Start at the outside edges and work into the centre. Apply two layers of grapes at the top to create a three-dimensional effect.

7 Attach the completed bunches of grapes to the trellis. Use a single strip of 5mm ($^1/_4$in) foam board under the small bunch and a double strip beneath the large bunch.

8 Finally, attach the leaves in position with blobs of silicone adhesive. Set the leaves at slight angles to create a more natural look. Vary the height of each leaf by using different thicknesses of foam strips.

Grapes

The finished sculpture effectively conveys a grapevine entwined on a wooden trellis through the use of shaping, incising and blocking. Handmade, cotton rag papers are always better to shape than wood pulp papers.

Finished size: (baseboard) 205 x 185mm (8 x 7¹/₄in)

Sea shells

Sea shells are ideal subjects for white-on-white paper sculpture. Their lovely flowing shapes and small intricacies are subtly defined through the natural light.

Finished size: approximately 150 x 75mm (6 x 3in)

Long-tailed wren

This tropical long-tailed wren makes a very frameable sculpture. The head and body have been kept very simple so as to emphasize the intricate detail of the wings and tail. The addition of a tiny coloured eye brings this sculpture to life.

Finished size: 100 x 175mm (4 x 7in)

Painting techniques

Water mill

It is often difficult to find plain papers of exactly the right colour or texture for a particular project. However, many papers can be embellished with extra colour using simple painting techniques. In this project of an old water mill, I demonstrate three techniques: applying a wash, for the sky and for the water passing over the mill wheel; spattering, to create texture on the walls of the buildings; and sponging, to achieve the running water effect in the millstream.

Large flat areas of paper, such as the walls and roof of the buildings are best supported on sheets of 3mm (⅛in) foam.

Check list

White watercolour paper and an assortment of colours of uncoated paper

Tracing paper and pencils

Scissors

Craft knife, steel ruler and cutting mat

Foam core board, 3 and 5mm (⅛ and ¼in) thick

PVA glue and cocktail sticks

Shaping tools and embossing mat

Set Square

Acrylic paints, brushes, old toothbrush, natural sponge and palette

Enlarge this diagram as required to make a working pattern.

40

1 Mix blue acrylic paint with water and stir thoroughly to remove every tiny spot of neat colour.

2 Cut an oversize piece of watercolour paper for the sky area and lay a wash of clean water over the surface.

3 While the water is still wet, lay in a wash of blue paint. Leave to dry, then trim to the size of the baseboard.

4 Paint a little of the sky colour on a piece of scrap paper. Pick some colour up with a natural sponge and work the sponge on to white paper. Allow to dry.

5 Use the tracing as a guide to find the best part of the sponged water, then use the tip of a craft knife to mark each end of the top edge.

6 Turn the paper over, pencil over the knife marks, then measure and mark the bottom edge. Cut the shape with a craft knife against a steel rule.

7 Mix olive green in a palette and take up some of the paint on an old toothbrush. Tap the brush on the side of the palette to remove excess paint.

8 Use a stiff piece of card or plastic against the bristles of the brush to spatter the paint over the walls of the buildings.

9 Glue the washed sky on the baseboard. Cut out and shape the edges of the two levels of trees; note how they extend well down the image area. Apply glue to their bottom edges and then assemble them on to the baseboard.

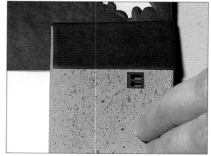

10 Cut out the shape of the right-hand building, extending it up across the roof and down below the stream. Crease along the roof line and glue the roof in position. Turn the shape over and glue a window frame over the window opening. Glue a piece of 3mm (⅛in) foam, cut slightly smaller than the size of the wall and with a cut out for the window, on the wall.

11 Stick an oversize piece of blue paper over the window cut out.

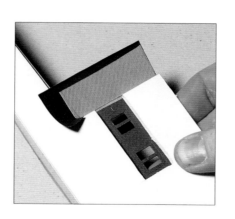

12 Glue a strip of 5mm (¼in) foam across the bottom of the building and then glue the completed building to the baseboard.

13 Make up the other two buildings in a similar way to that described in steps 10 and 11. For the centre building (with the chimney), cut the roof oversize on its length and tuck it in behind the chimney.

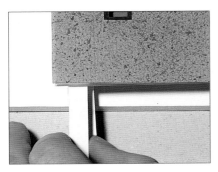

14 Glue the right-hand side of the centre building to the front surface of the first building. Support the left-hand side with a double strip of 5mm (¼in) foam.

15 Repeat step 14 for the third building; support its left-hand side with a triple strip of 5mm (¼in) foam.

16 Glue the stream in position. Use different layers of blocking to hold it parallel to the baseboard. Glue the water spray to the back of the millwheel. Attach small pieces of foam board to the centre and rim of the wheel and glue it to the building.

17 Build up layers of foam strips at the bottom left-hand corner of the picture to create a level just proud of the millwheel.

18 Glue a 3mm (⅛in) strip of foam behind the water chute, and then position it behind the millwheel. Glue the foreground foliage to the foam strips and finally, glue the tiny hub to the middle of the wheel.

Water mill

The finished sculpture clearly shows the washed sky, the spattered stonework and the sponged mill stream. Use your imagination and these painting techniques to embellish your own work.

Finished size: 275 x 215mm (10³/₄ x 8¹/₂in)

OPPOSITE

Waiting for the train

This painted scene is constructed entirely from white, cotton rag watercolour paper that has been coloured using various painting techniques. The finished effect is that of a three-dimensional watercolour painting. Vary the strength of the colour washes to achieve a wide range of beautiful velvety gradations.

Finished size: 175 x 270mm (7 x 10¹/₂in)

Explosion of toys

A child's Christmas dream – a multitude of colourful toys bursting through the white paper background. This piece was constructed using many different types of coated and uncoated papers. The stars were made using gold foil coated paper, to make them reflect light and add a sparkle to the design.

Finished size: 560 x 360mm (22 x 14in)

Index

Dove

This white-on-white image of a dove makes an ideal subject for a greeting card. When laid on a pastel base and mounted on a dark card, the contrast works well.

Finished size: 125 x 125mm (5 x 5in)